This Minute

POETS OUT LOUD PRIZE WINNERS

Lee Robinson
Hearsay, 2003

Janet Kaplan
The Glazier's Country, 2002

Robert Thomas
Door to Door, 2001

Julie Sheehan
Thaw, 2000

Jennifer Clarvoe
Invisible Tender, 1999

Jean Gallagher

This Minute

Fordham University Press New York 2005

Library of Congress Cataloging-in-Publication Data

Gallagher, Jean, 1962–
This minute / Jean Gallagher. — 1st ed.
p. cm.
ISBN 0-8232-2546-1 — ISBN 0-8232-2547-X (pbk.)
I. Title.
PS3607.A415435T48 2005
811'.6—dc22
2005016809

Printed in the United States of America
07 06 05 5 4 3 2 1 First edition

FOR MY TEACHERS:

Marie Ponsot
Janet Abels
and
David Sinclair Birdsell

Contents

Acknowledgments

Grateful acknowledgments to the editors of the volumes in which these poems first appeared:

Commonweal: "It Turns Out"; "Edge"; "The Life of the Verbs"; "Riches"; "The Untamed Thing"; "Two Math Lessons"; "Dream Fable of Horse and Fish"; "Nothing Seems to Happen. Everything Sails."

The Journal (Ohio State University): "Episodes in the History of Photography: Childhood, ca. 1903"; "Storyville Brothel, New Orleans, 1912"; "Bal Musette, 1931"; "Wall, Chicago, 1948."

And: heartfelt thanks and affection to Rosemary Deen and Scott Hightower, good friends to poets and poems.

This Minute

The Early History of Photography

The first photographer's sister spent the summer
watching the leaf-imprints disappear.
Just like life, she wrote to him, but a little slower;
like a chemical recipe for gratitude.

Shhh, the first photographer said, hovering
over the silver salts arrayed like listening devices.
Don't let the sun know what we're doing.
This is a god we can capture and he'll never know it,
never miss these little fistfuls of glitter, dumbed down.

Dear sister, you must know the miracle is in the stoppage.
Motion is cheap and plentiful;
standing still is what costs and costs.

Episodes in the History of Photography: Childhood, ca. 1903

(Jacques-Henri Lartigue)

I can't read yet but I still know that I am
something born for happiness   the flight
down stone steps   the air whistling the word *balustrade*
like something the troubadours hide in their purses.

The luckiest angels   the ones of gravity   lick my ears
like puppies. My cat jumps like a star.
My red ball lifts off   my nurse's
eyes aloft like a brand-new saint's.

Gravity is my own god   the one who lets me
trick him   the one who allows
everything   as long as everything lasts just a second
just enough for the clicking sound of my eye

giving way into the nothing   the glorious   the temporary
surrounding my flying   falling   leaping beloveds
who will never in my book die.

Two Math Lessons

Grade 3

What belongs with what and how
do you name it. Now that's a math
I can do, I thought, opening to page 1,
the very beginning, the first
white crocus in the season of idea.
The gaggle, the pride. The happiness of that,
the ease, the luxurious narrative possibilities
of the geese, the crows, the family of smiling lions.
Until page 2: the hard birth of abstraction,
the transparent knife too heavy and sharp to use.
The practically invisible, snippy awfulness of the minus sign.
The black, gut-punching spaces opening
in the multiplication table; the utter
damnability of 8 x 9.
Now I am an astronaut cut loose from the physical ship
in my deflating silver suit, losing something
vital with every float-away, go-away,
get-away second.

Grade 9

Returning, an alien life-form, fourteen, I fell
into the open hatch door marked *Factoring Out* and found
something to love: working it out unto zero,
the weightless satisfaction, the clicking lock
of *nothing more to do.*

Episodes in the History of Photography: Girlhood, ca. 1865

(Clementina, Lady Hawarden, and Her Daughters)

All our games are purposeful; all our costumes,
including the paper stars on our foreheads, actual.
In and out of mother's mind we work
as hard as any twelve apostles, playing
ourselves into the real, dressed up in
whatever will get us there, in time, in time.

The Adventures of This Minute

This minute enters gravity
and likes it, for a while.

This minute serves up something fiendish-yellow and
    hollow that whistles
straight over noon's net. The officials, the clockhands,
    clap and call it fair.

This minute, anybody's dog, never knows its owner's
answer to the question, *what kind?* But it guesses.

This minute, on a bender, seeks shelter in
orange. And blazes, tulip.

This minute hollers its name just to hear it bounce against
the glass and water walls of a single span of attention.

This minute, sealed in sleep's diving bell, dreams it can
    retrieve its lost ducks,
the arguments, from last week's blackish waters.

This minute drops what it can't use and then itself
like something burning, paper, words.

A Man in the Early Stages of Alzheimer's Disease Talks to His Twenty-Year-Old Daughter

And what's your name again the father says
and she sees all at once how the ocean enters everywhere
how the rib drifts from its cage
how the eyes   those fraternal twins   are parted
despite all the years in the womb holding hands
how the bones of the feet go their own way
how even the neurons must leave home at last just as she
is about to.

Miracles A and B

(Mark 5:21–43: Woman Stops Bleeding; Girl Rises from the Dead)

The girl has that bluish, waiting look
I used to have before I started running
out of myself in red erasable footprints.

She doesn't know the whole equation yet
for *missing*, she a single number waiting to be
added and divided on which side of the lesser-than.

Watch: she'll flicker and go under, the floating decimal point
in her face slipping into one of the gaps, the skipped
beats, the stitches kids that age sometimes

drop, knitting the world out of sugar and idea.
I'm standing entire outside the house
of what I was. The girl is dead.

She'll walk again in just a minute, but different:
she'll have lost the patient look, stepping
into the red shoes just becoming her size.

Field

Scratchy itchy twenty I said I want
To get my hands in the dirt of it where
Is the middle of my life.

Up to my knees in it now at forty what
Do I know but that even the middle is nothing but edge
After edge and my life is the place where the plow blade does
Its work that is my work.

Dream Fable of Horse and Fish

The horse I am runs deeper
and deeper into the city, willingly
trading the manifold wild for the one
common herb of manifold possible tastes.
Its mane still works in the breeze like before.

The fish, out of love for the horse,
hits the hard sidewalks and finds them
very hard indeed. I ask the fish
I am: are you so sure
you can give it up: the education,
the ambitions, the plans? The fish
cries and cries its water away.

Piero I: Myth of Instead

(Legend of the True Cross: The Death of Adam)

My father when he was dying scooped up a handful
of raw time and watched it glisten and drip.
Get rid of this, he said. *Find out*
what will work. So I went and knocked at the back
gate of the old man's suspicious, sumptuous past.
Waited, waited in the atemporal breeze.
What finally came to answer was dressed like an untouched
hour, still in its white wrapping. *Listen,*
I said, *here's what I need,* handing over
the list with just the one word on it. There was a silence
the exact length of my father's life. *There is*
no mercy like that, it finally said. *But here's*
what you get instead: appearance, disappearance, the one
green shoot. Plant it and get out of the way.

Episodes in the History of Photography: Storyville Brothel, New Orleans, 1912

(E.J. Bellocq)

Every ghost through here leaves a spill
yours the polite nowhere look and god's
own error on your shoulders asking *what*
is the future and where. Not yet scratched
in its mirror   I can tell you
    in the lightning run through my black stocking
    in the patent firestrap of my black shoe
    in the satin pillowful of money burning
    in the glass shawl I'll break to wear.
Thank you   you never fail to say and leave
its picture   splinters   on the bed.

Ovidian Prayer: On What Burns One Up

Desire for the genuine: the sun's original
Cadillac; the lover's true, light-struck
face. *I want it. I want it right*
now. Let my unfinished things
get born without me. Or the world
be set like a clock back to its dumb green
secret. Or let at least the moss get back
to work, cover up the scorch-marks.

Nothing Seems to Happen. Everything Sails.

Nothing seems to happen but the daily
swimmings and drownings and savings of this
bright, bound ocean. Everything in the room,
the room itself, sails the dense, clear current,
blue ship launching into the luck, future,
nowhere we might or might not have, into
what we assume, take on as if it had
weight and we were sure of veering out to-
gether into the rest of every day.

Episodes in the History of Photography: Mexico City, 1923–26

(Tina Modotti and Edward Weston)

1. *Portrait of Her Reciting*

In the prolonged exposure
                her voice accumulates
long vowels swinging
                consonants ticking
my audible life is there
                waiting for itself.
        Let it wait.

2. *Rooftop Photo Session*

The city below unpockets its harsh, sacred toys
for us, but up here I'm slick as platinum paper.
The roof tiles cook like little stoves at noon and you
lay me out on their perfect light with a silver
chloride blanket. It leaves a mark, a darkish sun:
that's me, leaving already for the big future.
Who is taking what, the picture wants to know.
My judas puppets, my patient holy piñatas—
all for smashing, all for keeps.

3. *Commission to Document Religious Images*

Juguete, angelito, unhappy wooden
god, don't forget me just because
I'm looking right at you and starting to know your names.

4. *Letter from California*

Blessed be nothing, she said, running
her hand along the shine. I turned it all
into idea, the better to own it, the better to travel.

5. *Rhyolite*

Someday I'll go to the desert and make the doorway
explicit. But I already know there is only
doorway, pure doorway, sometimes with a lovers's name.
It has other names, too: oxygen, rock. Open, locked.

Him Fishing

In this floating miniature kingdom
he is the dark upright among silver
horizontals—boat, lake, the invisible
fish he's coaxing like coins from a giant's pocket.
The pole bends double; his attention tightens like a lens.
The fish a sliver of shapely, unreadable thought;
his the solitude I've sworn out loud to protect.

Episodes in the History of Photography: The Invention of the Solarization Process, 1929

(Lee Miller and Man Ray)

In the darkroom his eyes rolled back like headlamps. That's
how he knew
he was seeing her. Oops, she said, spilling the light
out of its box, I thought you said *drop the pretense.*

You think I'll never leave you. I'll leave you
this: the body's bright edge brought back,
the light-struck negative of the place your eye has been taking
all night.
Blink or you'll miss it when I say *I'm right here, my love.*

This Minute Q & A

Q: What spicy get-up is this minute wearing now.
Q: What is it whispering inappropriately, privately.
Q: Whom is it wrapping in its gauzy scarves.
Q: What charming foreign city is it always leaving in its heart.
Q: Under whose bed does it leave its satin dancing shoes.

A: Nobody, nobody, nobody.
A: Every single sound.

Episodes in the History of Photography: Bal Musette, 1931

(Brassaï)

I. Promenade

Somewhere here is the secrecy of the open heart,
the hidden promenade of it, the whistle and shush, if
you have ears to hear. Otherwise the eye fills up
on desire's empty chemical lumens: the blinking,
scattershot surface of a whole, insular ocean.
The tuxedo girls, the two boys sharing
the one suit, the local butchers dancing
in their sleep awake in the roar of a great, sweet
privacy. What you see is the red satin herring,
the burnt-paper fancy dress between you
and what love looks like to itself.

II. Two Boys, One Suit

Lean way toward me, you with the seven habits
of holy fools. There's this to share: the skin
we made up and call *world.* Put your arms
way round me to find the difficult elements,
even the calcium, rocking themselves away
till the dust shines with us. What was the word
you just blew away like chalk? *Wish.*

Piero II: Itinerary

(The Queen of Sheba, on Her Way to Ask Solomon
Hard Questions, Encounters Something Surprising)

My luggage crammed with gold bribes and a list
of questions like a paper-clip necklace glittering
and scratching. There were numbers, I'd heard, that know God.
I'd come to study the math, but got no further
than banging my knees on the hard edge of *this,*
an opaqueness, an elementary bridge between what
and what. It looks solid, but keep looking:
the molecules whistle and spin; the little trap
doors in the atoms open and shut. As solid
as hydrogen but I'll have to walk on it anyway to drop
my passport in the water, let my picture unlock.
Is that what prayer is, unlearning the names of.

Episodes in the History of Photography: Lake George, NY, 1933

(Georgia O'Keeffe and Alfred Stieglitz)

Can I unload the lake's green light   would I
know where to look with the desert's magnets
pulling the blue metal in my eye.
I still know how to swim through your picture
of me   rock mermaid trailing silver
salt   crow's feet   married also
to this minute. Which of my two husbands
is it you   gives me love's later
invitation   *take leave freely.*
Can you picture now what I am taking   leaving
a kiss unhinged of all its water.

Ovidian Prayer:
On What Turns One into a Tree

Dread of another's pressing need or just
of time's usual, personal demands. *I don't*
want to. I don't want to at all. Let me
give away what I am by the roots. Or be what comes back
from a long falling-off. Or at least let what I drop
be an amber someone else can use.

Why Not Call It a Carriage Instead

Not exactly a mistake. Not so much
dropped as *let down*, like rope from the sailor's
hand. Didn't get very far down the multiplication
table, did you, little multiplier. And then
what happened, after the glue went
kerflooey, just like Heraclitus says it does?
But doesn't he also say: *what was scattered*
gathers. So what else have you gathered into, what else
has closed you a term in its fist? You were three
or four words leaving the body, express.
Where did you get spoken? On the way out.
What were the words? *On the way out.*

Heraclitus, *Fragments*, tr. Brooks Haxton, Viking, 2001

Episodes in the History of Photography: Honeymoon in Russia, 1942

(Margaret Bourke-White and Erskine Caldwell)

His equipment: One corduroy jacket. One ear-dictionary.
One blood-typewriter.
My equipment: Three thousand flashbulbs, individually
wrapped.
Eight cameras, one for each workday, one
for his dreams.
My eyes' heavy jewelry leaning toward the
magnets in his hair.
The war, both wars, the tripod I can't get
steady.

Ovidian Prayer: On What Turns One into Stone

The future coming at me with its claws
out. The mirror saying: did you
forget? *I want it to stop. I want it*
to stop for always. Let the statue of me
offer its arms to the snow. Let
the slow-mo of my heart get me nowhere.
Let it take forever and a day to get there.

This Minute's Stuff

In this minute's jewelry box
all the zero-shaped things
fit you like your very own numbers.

Peek open this minute's purse, built like a lung
to allow and allow: the compact between you and it,
the eye-sized mirror you know a little something in.

Rummage this minute's closet,
xylophoning the hangers of the future's fancy dresses
already given clean away.

This minute's medicine cabinet opens and shuts heartwise.
Its heart medicine tastes like the rough, dissolving salts
licked off your beloved's photograph.

Under this minute's bed you can juggle all you like.
Dust is no object but a process you can understand
with every cell of your juggling hand.

Slink past this minute's swap meet.
You can hear its familiar voice shouting
Up for grabs, all of it.

Ovidian Psalm: On What Turns One into a Bird

(Procne and Philomel)

The betrayer built into every cell; the trap-
door in all the sidewalks. Take what you want,
I'll never not tell, even when my tongue
makes way for the scissors of the empty air. Even
falling I'll still wear the story in red
letters on my shirt and everyone will know our real
name is fly-by-day, fly-by-night.

Piero III: Weight

(Solomon, Meeting the Queen in the Temple,
Acknowledges Certain Construction Problems)

> *And Solomon left all the vessels unweighed, because*
> *they were exceeding many: neither was the weight in*
> *the brass found out.* —I KINGS 7:48

Well, it is after all a kind of immortality,
the blank numbers riddling the house I built
to keep all this bright nothing in; the gilded
interior like a mind where the alphabetic noises go
at night. And, yes, always the one piece
that refuses, the resistant incalculable thing I can't
do anything with but hope for a while it holds my weight.

Episodes in the History of Photography: Paris Street, n.d.

(Eugène Atget)

Hold your eye open like god's: the people
come and go like breath, like fingerprints
in salt solution. The city is never
not under construction, but the houses
stay: patient animals, sleepers
turning, private and hard at work.

The waking have one world
in common. Sleepers
meanwhile turn aside, each
into a darkness of his own.

*

Even a soul submerged in sleep
is hard at work, and helps
make something of the world.

—Heraclitus, *Fragments*, tr. Brooks Haxton, Viking, 2001

Work

(Sayings of the Desert Fathers/Photographs of Robert ParkeHarrison)

1. *Of Humility*

Haven't you already disappeared.
Make it work.
Make it flower.

2. *Of Quiet*

Learn how to say: there is no one here besides me
        and the absolute noise.
I remember water, the pendulum
sound of it.

3. *That One Ought to Live Soberly*

The sky is too large and thoughts scatter like
        photons. Why I don't go outside.
The garden is plugged in so I
can keep my eyes down.

4. *Of Self-Restraint*

Some people can't handle the silence and insist
        on flying nowhere, nowhere.
Toward is the thing I like
to dream of best.

5\. *Of Love*

I live alone because of the single-mindedness of angels,
the thousand thousand white desert flies. Even
just one man has too many intentions, all of
them dear.
I bring a little something to the crash site and leave it
there. I am not disappointed.

6\. *That One Ought to Pray Without Ceasing*

Stay where you are and disappear a little more.
How far can this thing go. How far
can anything go.

7\. *Of Discretion*

Wear yourself down to nothing, you'll never be as jobless
as the angels, secure in their continual, invisible
churn. Maintain just sufficient hunger and work to
keep it alight.
Who made the world and then unmade it with light.
I ride my homemade bicycle in between.

8\. *Of Perfecting*

What is there left to do: become only fire.
I can build my way there
hammering on water.

9\. *Of Patience*

My thoughts rake me over.
Why does it seem that I am always just finishing
raking up what's left of the world.

10. *That One Ought Not to Possess Anything*

Forget your name, already empty.
I like the wasted look of things and that
is my kingdom.

11. *That Nothing Ought to Be Done For Show*

The secret life the only work. Hidden from what,
from whom.
No one can see me here, waiting between
the two bells, the pronouns.

12. *Of Fortitude*

I wove them for a year, and when my room got too
crowded, I burned them all and started again.
That's how much I need the work.
Yes, it is dirty, the work, but I only sometimes get tired flying
the preterite's stubborn, oxygenated kites.

13. *Of Contemplation*

Press this up against your heart: I am not here.
My contraptions flower. Even here
there is something.

The Life of the Verbs

begins when you feel it slow down and start stopping:
the grab-wheel, the what-if wheel,
the where-is-it wheel, the clench-wheel.
It slows down and undoes and what enters
is only the life of the verbs. Beginning with *open,*
beginning with *offer,* beginning again and again with *allow.*
The verbs whoosh through you, laughing like neutrinos,
asking *what are you made of?* Asking, exiting.

February

The look of a river just unfrozen. The history
of the solid world almost still-there.
The old hard legible. The syntax sprung.
The driftwood substantives dispersing down-
stream on silver transitives. Birds already
not-leaving traces. Already spring's
disappearances waiting to happen.

Cure

(Minor Characters from the Gospel of Mark)

Dumb spirit   deaf spirit   spirit dirt
  Muscles into all the rooms in my throat
  Throws my mind in the fire
  Holds my head under water too long.

Is it me   this bully   must be
  What else could so knot up my tongue's white cords
  Jam the upper roadways of my ears
  Lock down my eyes' cranky metal gates?

Be opened   does someone actually say it   and what
    do I see
  Men like trees walking
  Trees like men kissing
  Water like girls sleeping
  Girls like water talking.

It doesn't need to be any clearer   the way I've been
    always entire.

It Turns Out

It turns out that *no children* is the unlooked-
for adventure. My hours, unhooked,
breathing, from the blood machine, beat
and flutter like new little lungs and hearts
as seen by special sonography.

My hours, honorably discharged after
training for an 18-year war that never
happened, drop their rifles. How light, light,
stepping out of their like-new camo suits,
which, I gather, still let you be seen through to.

The life of my hours unbuckles into present tense.
I walk and walk in its bright blue shoes.

That the Gospels Are Motion Studies

Look at his continual busman's holiday: ferrying
himself and the multitudes from coast to salt-leprous
coast; jumpstarting the batteries in the lungs
left running overnight; setting the motors
in the stalled retinas whirring—Christ the roving
mechanic, rewiring the minute's moving parts.

Christ the method actor turns faster
than the speed of film. Even the extras jolt
into their cures, dropping frames on their way
to an anonymous, useful afterwards: *she rose*
and ministered unto them. He picked up his bed and went home.

The Untamed Thing

Allow somehow for the untamed thing.
Shy, slippery. Severed, whole, severe.
Who brought it? It brought itself,
as the ocean does and does. It brings itself.

You be the silent farmer playing up the ground
for its harrow music, made half of dirt
and half of the metal attentions, turning.
Skim off the *what you would.*
What's left is the untamed thing,
which you will forget, you can't help it, into its verbs.

This Minute Reads a Little New Testament at Bedtime

It always likes the miracle parts, the double axles
and triple lutzes on time's ice. Ten! Ten! Ten!
it shouts, holding up its score cards.
But it also like the lulls and pools in between,
the lexical acreage, the koans. *Hold still,*
it says to itself, *and let the Wisteria Sermon climb you.*
It never fails to get sad when things inevitably go to pieces—
the dumb cops, the smarmy prosecutors, the perp walk
leading always to the same last thirsty room.
But wait, wait. Something in purely reflective clothing
is well on its way. Something to point
to the emptied place and laugh its blinding laugh.
Wrapped up in that raiment, this minute puts out the light.

The Saints' Minute Calendar

Monday they wear this minute's rhinestones and
elbow-length lavender gloves.
Tuesday they ride this minute's faulty fire engine, whooping.
Wednesday they pole-vault the police barricades into this
minute's parking lot of roses.
Thursday they pirouette in this minute's wheelchair.
Friday they ignore the odd clicking sound under this
minute's hood and step on the gas.
Saturday they stay home and sew this minute's initials
into the collars of their flight suits.
Sunday they sleep in and pull this minute's covers over
their heads. The grammar of their dreams is nothing
but verbs and adverbs.

Edge

1.

Sit right at the edge, legs dangling
over. Learn to love the air's empty
decisions, having nothing to do with you.
Heels bouncing heartbeats off the cliff wall:
that's the edge. A little copper-colored
lightning braceletting the sky: that's chatter,
gone missing quickly in the cobalt. A few weedy
shrubs pushing out of the rock gaps, what
are they? Blood noise. The industry of breath.

2.

Did you know: the alleged edges and surfaces of things
consist of electromagnetic fields only.
Unplug them and your hand goes right through, nothing
much mixing with nothing much else. Physical,
but not the way you'd thought. Like that verb the human
heart: a heuristic for what? A helluvan appetite.

3.

Be opened, but don't tell anyone,
Christ kept saying. It spills over, however.
I can't not tell. *No edges* is my name
for God, while I must ride the raw edge,
the this-minute, the vegetal light, the *seems.*

Piero IV: Camera

(Constantine's Dream)

All night I can hear the world hum,
a refrigerator door left open somewhere, the cold
rush of *I promise you this* wasting itself

around the minor constellations. Something the color
of new ice silted up with an old idea
rockets into your dream: the one about

the war and no blood left under your nails,
the one in which everything tilts because of your weight.
I look straight into the camera. There is nothing to want.

Episodes in the History of Photography: Wall, Chicago, 1948

(Aaron Siskind)

I built my eye a house in the unmakings where
intention unzips its long silk coat and
lets out the accident it always carries   the soft
grenade in its heart pocket. Here the oxygen
blooms awry and here the water slides
its knife and here the forgiven local gods
walk their steadfast entropic walk   saying
there is no abandonment   just the varied
unending attentions   some personal   some
not. Here the goddess of the water stain
shakes the box of alphabets in her arms and says
come and get it.   Dust-letter   fire-
letter   let me read you while I can
silently first   then out loud.

Two Cities

I've come to think of them in terms of *throngs*,
of *hosts*, of biblically-proportioned gangs
of perpetual potentialities, massing and agitating
but light, like bubbles leaving boiling water.
An electron-weight urban populace, as densely arrayed
as the residents of Mexico City! Of Nairobi! Of Beijing!
Of midtown Manhattan at noontime, an almost corpuscular
jostling.

I've long lost sight, among those several billion bobbing heads,
of the one or two I used to harangue on the spirit phone:
Come on now, darling, please don't dawdle.
They're off spinning their spirit careers in the busy spirit city,
with spirit sweethearts and spirit apartments of their own.
Every so often, though, I do get a card,
handwritten fresh in grief's old vein-colored inks.
I read it over, drop it in the recycling bin,
look out the window at the biological city, and surprise myself
saying,
Thank you, who never did get born. Thank you
just the same.

The Natural History of This Minute

1. Its Minerals
Streaked with iron and salt, something
you can heft but can you get
inside it, the geode you'll have to break,
the handful of jacks you'll have
to scatter to know.

2. Its Vegetables
Lean in: you'll hear the conversion machines
heat up everything like love. You'll hear
the run of light's sugars and the eating of light's
bread. You'll hear them thinking and what they think
is: oh, so that's what you, your listening, sound like.

3. Its Animals
Like plants: geotropic, photo-
tropic, both at once, and with full assent.
Yes and yes, they say. They also sleep
their yes, asking without knowing: *just
a little more*. They keep inventing
the equation *I desire x* and the magnet
forward motion you are riding now.

Episodes in the History of Photography: Home, ca. 1970

(Diane Arbus)

Where am I at home   with the gravity-strafed
dirt saints   arriving at *now* gradually
in pieces   like identical triplets   woozy and grateful
with delay.   With the circus girl shiny with invisibility
swallowing nothing but her own platinum edge.
With the scandalous detailed christs turning
x into *y* because they know themselves well
enough.   *Come on*   I say in each one's ear.
Let's walk light's plank   its single
fraying footbridge.   Let's open the jack-knife
at its heart and be   like anyone
the specific errors of our ways.

What Sustains

Atmosphere. Under-lake.
The local stations of the more and less solid.
The doubts of the introspective centurions,
like intermittent nailheads in their porous faith,
providing the structural integrity, the narrative jolt.

Whatever it is, it also flirts away, skirts away, high heels
    spinning.
It plays, it mercies. Carries a crumpled, clean, summer-weight
    sadness
down at the bottom of its purse where the loose beads click
and the coins settle for nothing but themselves.

The riches of this nothing, the wastrel gleam of it.
The poor throat empty at its center, singing-saying: *feed.*

Riches

In the very midst of my riches,
the gold gravel silting up in the future's little corners,
I begin to wonder: where can I start to strip it?
How much can I set loose in the near-zero gravity
of whatever my life floats in, the aqueous, imageless
process I dream up as God's mind?

Let's see: no cat, no kids, no dog. But what about the man
ticking like fire beside me, the shining
track of privacy running parallel to mine?

Him I will love with my whole disappearing act.
Him I will love with the clock talking its trash in my throat.
Him I will love the length of my unspooling ordinal numbers.
Him I will love jangling the bracelets of minutes stacked
all the way, all the way, up both arms.

Red Canoe

Be what we are   a goings-on going where.
Easily upset   readily uprighted.
Be the lesson we are sworn and built to learn
  how to borrow lightness faithfully until we
  are it.

Episodes in the History of Photography: Shell, 1990

(Aaron Rose)

What are the verbs of the place: the eye's mercury
slide down the ossicular sheen, the vertebral
silk. The slide of everything you love
along the calcium road, the solarized road.

Every object here a purse full
of minutes, the purse with the rip in its seam. What
you see is the spill, gold dust and tin dust. The sound
would be that of a single heart in its cartilage, yours.

Ovidian Love Poem

Baucis saw Philemon come into leaf,
and Philemon saw Baucis put forth leaves.
Then . . . while it was allowed them,
they spoke and answered one another's speech . . .
(*OVID*, METAMORPHOSES, *BOOK V*)

Love let us see the tree in each other
speak this minute's green speech
our mouths the oak & linden
leaves they were always bent on being.

Ovid, *Metamorphoses*, tr. Charles Martin, Norton, 2004

What to Do with This Minute

Turn this minute loose.
No fingerprints, no marks.
No black paint carrying your name
or the name you think this minute endures.
This minute is without its name and itching to be gone.
And you, to live it, let it.

Like That

Any of night's rushing
edgeless noises—rain,
traffic, wind—can do it:
unbraid me from the hard knot,
the hook knot, the gut-punch
wakeup that remembers
its lead medicine: *this ends.*
How does it work? The way a shirt
left out in the rain for years
becomes rain. Becomes years.
Becomes what unmakes it
in every axle of fabric, x
by x. So each pixel
of listening loosens, flickering,
blinking: a field of
losing, alight. Let me
be undone by everything like that.

Cambium

1. In botany, the layer of tissue between the bark and wood, from which new wood and bark develop.

Remarkable, isn't it, that we've imagined a right
to *pursue happiness,* pursue it like the bad god
after the girl who'd rather be a tree
than give over. So pursue the tree. Pursue
the leaves. Pursue the bark beneath which
lies the little lab of change, unseen, making and
making and bringing the new out of nothing,
it seems, but itself. *From where, from*
where, I want to know, my pursuit seized up
and my hand at something like rest on the bark that bites me.

2. A bodily fluid formerly supposed to repair waste of tissue.

It's that *formerly supposed* that breaks my heart a little:
another good idea we had to give up.
But as for the heart, does it not in fact
waste a bit, if not break, and what else
does the repairs but our good and ultimately unworkable
ideas: the Dutch kid's finger keeping
back the watery end of the world?

3. An exchange of property.

I was never much for volleyball, especially all that
slapping up against the tender skin
of the inner forearms—whose idea was it
to have it sting so much? But even I can see
the implications of a game in which *to have* and *to give*
away are a single motion. *Spike it!* I hear
my teammates shouting. *Spike it straight*
into everyone else's emptying hands.

Piero V: Invention

(Torture of the Prisoner and *Discovery of the True Cross)*

1.

I threw my heart, stuffed with its alien intelligence,
down a well: *tell me.* I pulled my heart,
that starveling, up by the hair: *tell me where*
you buried it, the last of the genuine thing.

2.

I kept thinking: this can't be it, the leftover
junk of all the everyday torments. How
will I know it from the plain geometry of the clenched hand
opening always at last against its will?

3.

I'd imagined when I found it the world would spin shut,
perfected as a gold egg. But my invention crashed
and sputtered in its carbon arc, like the too-bright
precision accident of any particular life.

4.

Later, the nails, the last ideas, floated up
empty as new syringes. I melted them down,
mixed them in with all the other gleaming,
stubborn insistences. All but one, which I threw
in the sea: *give your inventions away.*

GIVING

A Bible Study Wordbook for Kids

by Richard E. Todd

This Wordbook Belongs To . . .

WingSpread Publishers
Chicago, Illinois